FASHION
TREASURES OF THE
MUSEUM OF FINE ARTS
BOSTON

Fashion

TREASURES OF THE MUSEUM OF FINE ARTS BOSTON

TEXT BY
ALLISON TAYLOR

A TINY FOLIO™
Museum of Fine Arts, Boston
Abbeville Press Publishers
New York London

Front cover and pp. 302–3: Isabel Toledo, American (born in Cuba), 1961–2019, *"Wave" dress*, 2011, silk plain weave (taffeta).

Back cover: European. *Pair of women's shoes*, 1750–1760s. Silk satin figured, embroidered with metallic thread, metallic galloon, leather and silk lining, leather sole.

Back endpapers (detail): Designed by Maurice Dufrène, French, 1876–1955. *Length of furnishing fabric*, c. 1927. Rayon and cotton jacquard.

p. 2 and front endpapers (detail): Italian, *Woman's court dress and petticoat (robe a la Francaise)*, c. 1775, silk taffeta brocaded with silk and metallic threads.

p. 6: *Mr. Rowe with Miss Wetherby's Class in the Egyptian Galleries, Museum of Fine Arts, Boston, 1910*. Photograph © Museum of Fine Arts, Boston.

p. 12: English, *Pair of gloves*, early seventeenth century, leather embroidered with silk, seed pearls, metallic threads, and spangles, trimmed with metallic bobbin lace and silk and metallic ribbon.

p. 34: French or Italian, *Stomacher*, late seventeenth–early eighteenth centuries, silk plain weave embroidered with metallic threads.

p. 70: American, *Man's two-piece suit*, 1810–20, wool twill (broadcloth).

p. 104: American, *Woman's dress*, c. 1856–58, silk plain weave (taffeta), trimmed with silk fringe tassels, machine embroidered net, bobbin lace.

p. 126: American, *Day dress*, c. 1870, silk plain weave (taffeta) and velvet, trimmed with silk fringe.

p. 148: Sorosis, American, *Pair of woman's shoes*, 1910–20, gilt leather, beads, rhinestones.

p. 194: Designed by Yves Saint Laurent, French (born in Algeria), 1936–2008, for House of Christian Dior, French, founded 1946, *Woman's dress "Bonne Conduite,"* Spring–Summer 1958, mohair and silk plain weave.

p. 232: Madame Grès, French, 1903–1993, *Evening dress*, French (Paris), 1962, silk knit (jersey).

p. 280: Designed by Olivier Theyskens, Belgian, b. 1977, for House of Rochas, French, founded 1925, *Woman's evening dress*, French (Paris), Spring/Summer 2005, silk plain weave, feathers.

CONTENTS

INTRODUCTION

In 1877, the Museum of Fine Arts, Boston, received its first gift of costume: an eighteenth-century brocaded court gown donated by the Italian art dealer Alessandro Castellani. As was standard practice at the time, the dress was cataloged as a "brocade" according to the technique of its fabric, and not as an example of period costume. At the time of the Museum's founding in 1870, its textile collecting efforts were focused on providing inspiration for designers in the local textile industry, rather than considering textiles and fashion as objects of fine art themselves, as they are today. Despite the Museum's early collecting efforts, it was not until 1930 that the Department of Textiles was officially established to house the ever-expanding collection of textiles and costumes.

While the place of costume within the institution was discussed as early as 1880, when a proposal to establish a historic costume collection appears in the Museum's trustee ledgers, it wasn't until 1933 that the MFA agreed to host a loan exhibition of American costumes organized by the Colonial Dames of Massachusetts. The first Curator of Textiles, Gertrude Townsend, noted that the "exhibition of costumes . . . would undoubtedly be interesting." That same year, Townsend rejected the proposed donation of a Worth gown, noting that her understanding of the Museum's collections policy only allowed for the acquisition of "such costumes whose material either as an example of weaving, embroidery, or lace, would have a place in the collection." It was Townsend, however, who would eventually bring in two significant gifts of Western costume and accessories, thereby establishing the fashion collection at the MFA.

The first of these donations was the Lehman Collection, given by Phillip Lehman in 1938 in honor of his late wife, Carrie Lehman. The Lehman Collection comprises over 350 textiles and costume accessories from the sixteenth to eighteenth centuries, including many fine examples of embroidery.

The second significant collection was given in 1943 by Elizabeth Day McCormick, a donation that immediately transformed the MFA's costume collection into one of the foremost in the country. (She was related to the inventors of the McCormick Reaper, a device that transformed American agriculture in the nineteenth century.) McCormick learned embroidery at a young age and developed a passion for it, becoming a collector not only of embroidery, but also of fine examples of eighteenth- to early nineteenth-century costume, accessories, and fashion plates—nearly 5,000 pieces in total. With this donation, the Museum began to recognize that costume was an increasingly significant part of the collection which could help support the emerging American ready-to-wear industry, although it would be another thirty-five years before the Department of Textiles added the word "Costume" to its title.

Prior to mounting an exhibition featuring the Elizabeth Day McCormick Collection in 1945, Townsend invited representatives of the American ready-to-wear industry for a private viewing, with such noted members of the industry as Adele Simpson, Nettie Rosenstein, Lily Dache, and Diana Vreeland attending. The timing of the donation of the McCormick Collection coincided with the establishment of the Costume Institute at the Metropolitan Museum of Art, the Fashion Wing at the Philadelphia Museum of Art, and the creation of the Design Laboratory at the Brooklyn Museum. At the same time, with the Second World War limiting contact with Europe, American designers and retailers across the country were beginning to emerge from the shadow of Paris and New York as important centers for ready-to-wear. The McCormick gift inspired several other donors to make substantial gifts of costume which signficantly grew the collection, including many examples of nineteenth-and early twentieth-century garments by designers such as Charles Frederick Worth, and contemporary designs, such as a 1930s evening gown by Elizabeth Hawes and a 1946 dress by Madame Eta, the latter inspired by a statue in the MFA's collection.

Gertrude Townsend was succeeded by Adolph Cavallo in 1959. Unlike his predecessors, Cavallo strongly promoted fashion as an art form equal to painting, sculpture, and architecture. The 1963 exhibition, *She Walks in Splendor: Great Costumes, 1550–1950*, was the first by a major American art museum to present fashion as art. In the catalog accompanying the exhibition, Cavallo made the case for acknowledging the artistry of fashion, "there is some constant quality, some inherent merit in the designer's handling of line, shape and color that transcends superficial considerations of fashion and lends the favored raiment the esthetic validity of a good painting or sculpture." Cavallo noted that tailors, dressmakers, and fashion designers—like any other artist—employ line, form, texture, and color to create objects of beauty and expressiveness, while also adding the unique element of movement.

In 1981, the department's name was finally changed to the Department of Textiles and Costume. Cavallo's successors made important acquisitions by designers such as Gilbert Adrian, Norman Norell, and Yves St. Laurent for Dior, and the first purchases (rather than donations) of twentieth-century costume. Each of these acquisitions was made for its aesthetic qualities, the importance of the designer, its provenance, or to fill gaps in the collection. Over the next several years, exhibitions such as *The Well-Dressed Eighteenth Century Man*, the only exhibit in the Museum's history to focus exclusively on menswear, and *Boston à la Mode: Fashionable Dress 1760s–1960s*, showcased the richness and depth of the MFA's fashion holdings. Finally, in 2000, the department's name changed to the Department of Textile and Fashion Arts, which it carries today. The change was made to "better reflect its [the department's] focus and direction."

Today the MFA's fashion and textile collection extends to some 55,000 objects, and continues to grow. The current focus is on collecting fashion that explores technology and innovation, as well as an effort to acquire more menswear, significant works by twentieth-century haute couture designers, and works by contemporary and emerging designers. The recent exhibition, *Gender Bending Fashion*, explored both the beauty and social relevance of fashion and self-expression in society. The depth and breadth of the Museum of Fine Arts' fashion collection provides a means to explore the beauty of fashion as art, while also investigating its social and historical importance. This book provides a glimpse of the collection's highlights, while giving readers an overview of the evolution of Western fashion over the centuries.

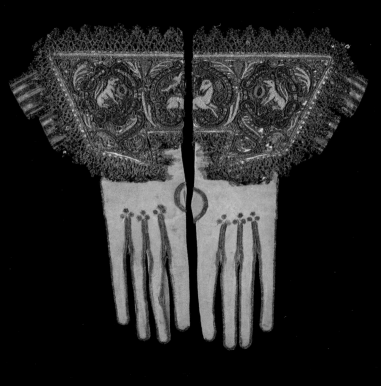

17TH CENTURY

Before the advent of industrialized production, textile materials were produced entirely by hand and were very expensive. Fine apparel and accessories, such as those featured here, were the province of the upper class who wore custom-made, elaborately decorated clothing which served as a powerful display of wealth and position. Few museums have examples of complete garments that date before the eighteenth century; the preciousness of expensive textiles led to garments being restyled or repurposed. Additionally, fabrics tore, became stained, or simply wore out. Much of what we know about clothing styles from the seventeenth century has been gleaned from painted portraits and fashion prints that began to appear in this era.

The formal clothing of both men and women tended to be highly structured, with boning, padding, or undergarments such as stays and hoops (called "farthingales") providing support and a display surface for the expensive textiles. Women's bodices were longwaisted at the beginning of the century, but waistlines rose over time, then descended back to the natural waistline by midcentury. Long, tight sleeves became fuller over the period, and often featured slashing to reveal linens worn beneath. Unfitted gowns, sometimes called nightgowns, with long hanging sleeves, short open sleeves, or no sleeves at all, were worn over the bodice and skirt and tied with a ribbon sash at the waist.

In the first part of the century, men's doublets (a type of jacket) were pointed at the waist and fitted close to the body, with tight sleeves. As with women's fashions, gradually waistlines rose and sleeves became fuller, and both body and upper sleeves might be slashed to show the shirt beneath. By 1640, doublets were loose, and might be open at the front to show the shirt. Short cloaks or capes, usually hip length, often with sleeves, were worn by fashionable men, usually slung artistically over the left shoulder, even indoors. Men's leg coverings, called hose, gradually gave way to more loosely fitting breeches, which ended at the knee. In the court of Charles II of England (1630–1685), men were required by royal decree to wear a long coat, a vest called a petticoat (which later became known as a waistcoat), breeches that gathered at the knee, a cravat, and wig. This uniform became the suit—coat, waistcoat, and breeches—the standard for men's formal wear.

The MFA's collection of seventeenth-century fashion includes many wonderful examples of costume accessories such as gloves, muffs, shoes, and handbags featuring intricate embroidery and beading. Many of these examples came to the museum as part of the Carrie Lehman and Elizabeth Day McCormick collections which were donated to the MFA in 1938 and 1943–44, respectively.

Italian. *One of a pair of women's chopines,*
late seventeenth–early eighteenth century.
Silk-cut velvet with giltmetal lace trim and linen lining, silk satin
ribbon, metallic woven trim, metal nails, wood, leather.

Italian (Venetian). *Pair of women's platform shoes (chopines)*, 1590–1610.
Tooled leather over wood with metallic braid.

Cortegiana Veneta

Pietro Bertelli, Italian (Paduan),
active late sixteenth–early seventeenth centuries. *Diversarum
nationum habitus . . . Apud Alciatum Alcia et P. Bertellium,* 1589.
Engraving with hand-applied color, 4½ × 3¼ in. (11.2 × 8.2 cm).   17

Italian. *Pair of children's shoes, or sample shoes*, 1610–20.
Tooled leather and silk tassels.

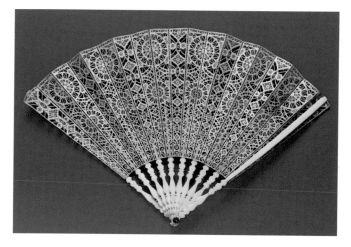

Italian or French. *Découpé folding fan*, c. 1590–1600.
Carved ivory sticks and cut parchment;
leaf with silk plain weave and mica inserts.

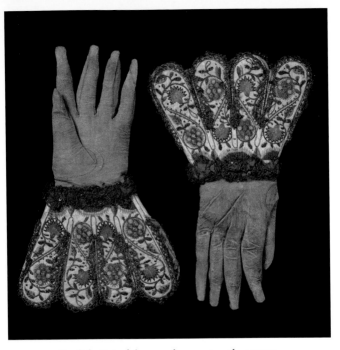

English. *Pair of gloves*, early seventeenth century.
Leather embroidered with silk, metallic threads, spangles;
metallic bobbin lace and silk ribbon.

Michiel Jansz. van Mierevelt, Dutch, 1566–1641.
Portrait of a Young Lady, 1617.
Oil on panel, 44½ × 33⅞ in. (113 × 86 cm).

21

English. *Woman's jacket*, c. 1610–15, with later alterations.
Linen plain weave, embroidered with metallic
threads and spangles; metallic bobbin lace.

English. *Drawstring bag*, late sixteenth–early seventeenth centuries.
Linen plain weave embroidered with silk, silver-and-gold
metallic threads; braided silk and metallic cords and tassels. 23

Abraham Bosse, French, 1604–1676, after Jean de Saint Igny, French, c. 1600–1649. *La Noblesse françoise à l'église* (set of 13 plates), plate 8, c. 1630. Etching and engraving on white laid paper, inserted into modern paper, 6 × 3¾ in. (15.2 × 9.6 cm).

Abraham Bosse, French, 1604–1676, after Jean de Saint Igny, French, c. 1600–1649. *La Noblesse françoise à l'église* (set of 13 plates), plate 9, c. 1630. Etching and engraving on white laid paper, inserted into modern paper, 5⅞ × 3¾ in. (15 × 9.6 cm).

Anthony van Dyck, Flemish, 1599–1641.
Isabella, Lady de La Warr, c. 1638.
Oil on canvas, 84 × 54 in. (213.4 × 137.2 cm).

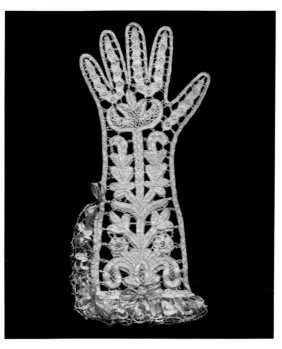

Italian. *Woman's bobbin lace glove*, c. 1650–1700.
Linen bobbin lace and silk ribbons.

Possibly Italian. *Pair of women's "slapsole" shoes*, c. 1670.
Leather, silk satin with straw appliqué, silk laces
and tassels, leather lining and sole.

Possibly Italian. *Man's shoe*, 1650–60.
Leather, wood, reproduction bow.

Nicolas Walraven van Haften, Dutch, 1663–1715.
Portrait of a Family in an Interior, c. 1700.
Oil on canvas, 18¼ × 21⅞ in. (46.4 × 55.5 cm).

French. *Muff*, c. 1680–90. Silk satin, embroidered with silk and metallic threads, hand painted, trimmed with silk ribbon and metallic bobbin lace.

English. *Child's coat*, 1710–50.
Cotton plain weave embroidered with cotton
and silk, trimmed with silk plain weave.

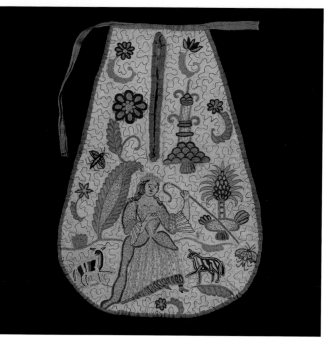

English. *Pocket*, early eighteenth century.
Cotton plain weave embroidered
with silk, trimmed with silk tape.

33

Sumptuous fabrics, wide skirts, and a conical bodice shape characterize women's fashions of the eighteenth century. Advances in the textile industry, and the expansion of trade between Europe and the Far East, led to an explosion of innovative and highly decorative textile designs. The beauty and complexity of textiles, particularly patterned silks, greatly influenced clothing design in this period, especially women's dresses in the first half of the eighteenth century.

For formal occasions in the early part of the century, women wore a dress called a *mantua*, made of silk or fine wool, with an open front, a train, and a matching petticoat. The train was worn looped over the hips to reveal the petticoat. The bodice was shaped by stays stiffened with whalebone, and skirts were supported by a hooped petticoat. Elbow-length sleeves ended in wide cuffs.

The mantua evolved to other relatively simple styles that showcased lengths of beautiful and expensive fabrics: the *robe volante*, a loose-fitting, draped gown, with pleats at both the back and front, and the *robe à la française*, also known as the *sacque* (or sack) gown, probably the most iconic silhouette of the eighteenth century. The *sacque* featured pleated panels of fabric that draped from the shoulders to the hem at the back and was worn over side hoops, or *panniers*; it remained the style of choice for formal occasions for much of the century. By the end of the century, cotton and lighter silks became fashionable and dress styles evolved to suit them. The *robe à l'anglaise* was similar in shape to the *robe à la française* but featured a tight-fitting back rather than draped pleats. The last few decades of the century saw the pannier replaced by "bum" or "rump" pads that moved the fullness from the sides to the rear. The *robe à la polonaise*, popular in the 1770s and 1780s, featured a skirt draped into three portions over a petticoat or underskirt of matching or contrasting fabric. Like many fashions of the period, it received its name from a current event—Poland was partitioned into three parts in 1772 and its territory divided between Russia, Austria, and Prussia. Bodices were typically open at the front, and were filled in with a stomacher, a triangular panel of fabric that covered the stays and was fastened in place with straight pins or hooks. Stomachers could be of the same fabric as the dress, but were often highly decorative, embroidered or embellished with lace or ribbon. The *compere* bodice, or false waistcoat, attached at the center with buttons or other fastenings.

Menswear typically consisted of a suit of three parts: the waistcoat, jacket, and breeches. Men's suits were made primarily of silks, velvets, and brocades. Woolens were used for the middle class and for sporting costumes. Waistcoats and jackets often featured ornate embroidery or lace decoration. Wide-brimmed hats turned up on three sides, called tricorns, were worn throughout the era.

English. *Pair of women's tie shoes*, 1725–50. Silk taffeta
with silk embroidery, silk binding tape, silk, linen
and leather lining, leather sole.

Robert Feke, American, c. 1707–1751.
Isaac Winslow, c. 1748.
Oil on canvas, 50 × 40⅛ in. (127 × 101.92 cm).

American (English fabric). *Man's sleeved waistcoat*, 1720s. Silk damask, brocaded with silk and metallic yarns, trimmed with gold metallic braid, lined with linen plain weave and silk plain weave (taffeta).   39

French. *Dress and petticoat (robe volante)*,
c. 1730–40. Silk lampas.

English, for the Spanish market. *Mask fan*, 1740s.
Paper leaf patched with parchment, etched, engraved, and painted
in watercolor; pierced, partially painted, varnished and
gilded ivory sticks; mother-of-pearl, brass.

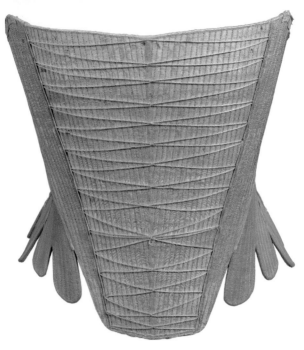

American. *Stays*, 1740–60.
Silk plain weave (tafetta moiré), linen plain weave, baleen.

Probably French. *Petticoat*, mid-eighteenth century.
Silk plain weave, quilted; silk ribbon binding and linen tapes.

French. *Man's negligee cap*, mid-eighteenth century.
Linen plain weave embroidered silk; silver braid edging.

John Singleton Copley, American, 1738–1815.
Nicholas Boylston, c. 1769.
Oil on canvas, 50⅛ × 40 in. (127.32 × 101.6 cm).

English. *Earrings*, 1750–1800.
Gold metal and *coque de perle*.

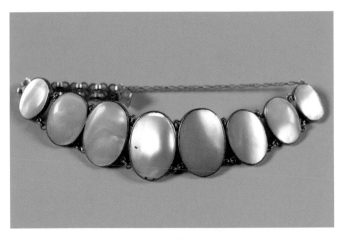

English. *Bracelet*, c. 1783.
Mother-of-pearl and gold.

Possibly American. *Apron*, eighteenth century.
Cotton plain weave embroidered with linen.

John Singleton Copley, American, 1738–1815.
Dorothy Quincy (Mrs. John Hancock), c. 1772.
Oil on canvas, 50⅛ × 39⅝ in. (127.32 × 100.65 cm).

French. *Woman's dress (robe á la française)*, 1760s. Silk satin weave with weft patterning floats *(faconée)*, silk plain weave with discontinuous patterning wefts (taffeta), silk plain weave, linen plain weave.

European. *Women's shoes*, 1760s–1770s.
Printed alum-tanned leather, applied colors, wood heel.

Possibly English. *Man's shoe buckles*, c. 1770.
Steel and white paste.

Probably French. *Man's three-piece suit*, c. 1750,
altered in the mid-nineteenth century.
Silk, voided and cut polychrome velvet, brocaded with silk.

French. *Dress and petticoat (robe à la française)*, c. 1770.
Silk cannellé patterned with weft floats and brocaded with silk thread.

French. *Man's formal suit,* 1770–80.
Silk satin, embroidered with silk.

Western European. *Stays*, 1770–90.
Linen plain weave, baleen, silk tape.

TAILLEUR COSTUMIER ESSAYANT UN COR A LA MODE.

Il est vêtu d'un habit noisete à collet noir de velours, dreté boutonniere d'or, les boutons et boutonnieres de l'habit de même, une veste de tricot crisée avec une très modeste, culotte de velours noir, et bas de soie gris: la jeune personne n'a qu'en simple jupon et des bas blancs, et l'on voit couvert de batiste trinte ou jamais.

Aprouvé Avec Privilege et Enregistré rue St. Jacques à la Ville de Coutances. A.P.D.R.

Designed by Pierre Thomas LeClerc, French, c. 1740–99, engraved
by Nicolas Dupin, French, published by Esnauts et Rapilly, French,
eighteenth century. *Gallerie des Modes et Costumes Français . . .*, 1778.
Hand-colored engraving on laid paper.

Possibly Dutch. *Woman's formal dress (robe á la française)*, c. 1735,
dress restyled, c. 1770. Silk satin with supplementary
discontinuous silk and metallic patterning wefts.

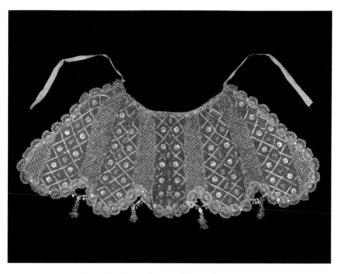

French. *Apron*, late eighteenth century.
Metallic thread lace embroidered with metallic thread,
trimmed with metallic bobbin lace and tassels.

Marie Louise Elisabeth Vigée Le Brun, French, 1755–1842.
Study of a Woman. Red chalk, 9½ × 5⅞ in. (24.1 × 15 cm).

French. *Dress and petticoat (robe à la polonaise)*, c. 1785,
altered at a later date. Cotton plain weave, block printed.

English or French. *Dress and petticoat (robe a l'anglaise)*, c. 1784.
Silk plain weave rib.

Designed by François Louis Joseph Watteau, French, 1758–1823, engraved by Pierre Adrien Le Beau, French, 1748–1800, French, eighteenth century. *Gallerie des Modes et Costumes Français . . . ,"* 1784. Hand-colored engraving on laid paper, 15 × 10 in. (38.1 × 25.4 cm).   65

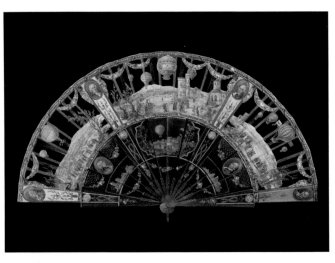

French. *Folding fan depicting scenes from the history of ballooning*, c. 1785.
Reformed protein (molded horn) sticks and
parchment leaf painted with gouache.

French. *Pair of women's beaded mules*, c. 1794. Glass beads (sablé),
leather sole and heel, silk lining, gilt metal trim.

American. *Wedding dress*, c. 1799. Dress: silk satin, embroidered with silk and metallic thread, silk plain weave trim. Petticoat: cotton plain weave embroidered with silver metallic thread.

Rowland Parry, American, active c. 1790–96, James Musgrave,
American, active 1792–c. 1813, Jeremiah Boone, American,
active c. 1790–96. *Mourning pendant brooch*, 1792. Gold, watercolor
on ivory, hair, glass, 2¼ × 1⅞ × ½ in. (5.7 × 4.8 × 1.3 cm).

EARLY 19TH CENTURY
1800–1845

Political revolutions in America and Europe, and the industrial revolution, helped ignite upheavals in fashion in the early nineteenth century. The silhouette of women's dresses from 1800 to 1810 differed markedly from the previous century—high waistlines, low necklines, and narrow skirts strongly influenced by classical sculpture was the norm. Sheer white muslin was the preferred fabric for evening wear, and while some form of corset was still worn to shape the torso, it functioned more to support the bust than to slim the waist.

By the 1820s, the waistline began to lower, allowing for more ornate decoration on the bodice and a return to tighter lacing. The narrow waist was balanced by wider shoulders and fuller skirts. Historical nostalgia continued to influence styles, with full skirts, ruffs and "vandyked" pointed lace collars, and slashed-and-puffed sleeves recalling the seventeenth century. Enormous puffed sleeves, supported by sleeve puffers, reached such large proportions that the sleeve volume eventually moved to the lower part of the arm, and by the 1840s, sleeves had reverted to a straight, simple cut. Technological developments in dye chemistry and textile printing made colorful printed textiles more accessible, and the heavy ornamentation of the 1820s decreased to allow textiles to become the focus once again.

Britain's Queen Victoria, crowned in 1837, strongly influenced fashion. The 1840s saw a return to softer colors and a modest silhouette reflecting increasingly popular social values of virtue and decorum for women. Skirts became wider—they were held out by as many as six petticoats—and were eventually supported by the early crinoline, which was stiffened with horsehair. Waistlines were narrow, tightly corseted under longer, rigid bodices. To balance wider skirts, larger hats and bonnets with elaborate embellishment became popular.

This period saw the final abandonment of lace, embroidery, and other embellishment from men's clothing outside of formalized court dress, not appearing again until the 1960s. Cut and tailoring developed into the key indicators of quality and style as wool became the dominant fabric for menswear. Breeches became longer, eventually being replaced by pantaloons or trousers. Cutaway coats with long tails behind and high collars were fashionable from 1800 to 1810. By the mid–1820s, the ideal silhouette for men mimicked that for women: broad shoulders with slightly puffed sleeves helped emphasize a narrow waist, often achieved with the aid of a girdle or belt, the masculine equivalent of stays or corsets. By the 1830s, calf-length, often double-breasted frock coats began to replace tailcoats for fashionable men.

American. *Woman's tunic*, c. 1801.
Linen plain weave embroidered with silk and metallic thread,
satin inserts and ribbon, linen plain weave lining.

French. *Bonnet*, 1800–05.
Silk net, silk satin ribbon, silk flowers.

Gilbert Stuart, American, 1755–1828.
Mrs. Thomas Bartlett (Hannah Gray Wilson), c. 1805.
Oil on panel, 28⅞ × 23½ in. (73.34 × 59.69 cm).

French. *Man's court suit*, c. 1805–8.
Wool broadcloth and silk satin embroidered with
silk and metallic threads, spangles, glass.

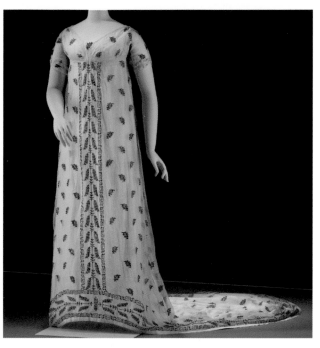

French. *Formal dress,* 1805.
Cotton gauze; embroidered with wool and cotton.

French. *"Demi Parure,"* plate 588 from *Journal des Dames et des Modes, Costumes Parisienes*, 1805. Etching with hand-applied color on laid paper, 7¾ × 4¾ in. (19.7 × 12.1 cm).

English. *Hat*, c. 1800. Silk plush, paper,
glazed-linen lining, silk braid.

Adèle Romany, French, 1769–1846.
Joseph-Dominique Fabry Garat Playing a Lyre Guitar, c. 1808.
Oil on canvas, 51¼ × 39½ in. (130.2 × 100.3 cm).

Indian (used in America). *Handkerchief*, early nineteenth century.
Printed cotton plain weave (block printed).

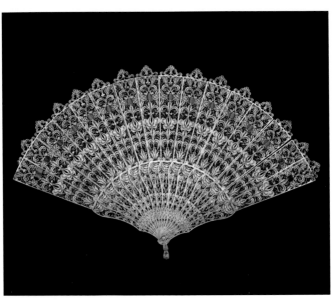

Possibly Russian. *Brisé fan owned by Marie Louise Bonaparte,*
second quarter of the nineteenth century.
Silver filigree blades with silk ribbon.

French. *Dress*, c. 1805.
Cotton plain weave; embroidered with cotton.

French. *Shell-shaped bag*, 1810–30. Linen plain weave embroidered with glass beads, leather, steel-and-silk cord.

Probably American. *Reticule*, c. 1800.
Silk plain weave, stenciled, hand-painted.

LES MODES ANGLAISES A PARIS

Le Suprême Bon Ton. N.º 22.

A Paris chez Martinet, Libraire, rue du Coq

Déposé à la Direction Gle

Published by Martinet, French, eighteenth–nineteenth centuries.
"Les Modes Anglaises à Paris" Le Suprême Bon ton, N.º 22, French, 1810–15.
Etching with hand-applied color, 11½ × 16½ in. (29.2 × 41.9 cm).

French. *Man's beaver hat*, c. 1810.
Beaver felt with silk grosgrain ribbon.

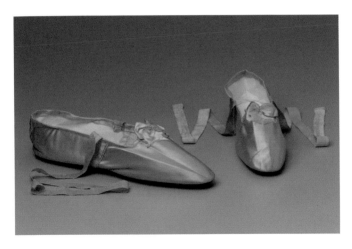

Probably French, worn in America. *Pair of woman's slippers*, c. 1815–25.
Silk satin, silk plain weave ribbon and binding,
leather, linen plain weave lining.

Possibly French, worn by Mehetable Stoddard Sumner (Welles),
American, 1784–1826. *Woman's dress*, 1815–20.
Silk net (tulle), silk satin trim, silk cord, wool embroidery.

Chapeau de paille d'Italie pardessus à la Chinoise.

Designed and engraved by Emile Jean Horace Vernet
(called Horace Vernet), French, 1789–1863. Drawing by Gatine, French.
Incroyables et Merveilleuses, Nº 16, 1813. Etching with hand-applied color,
$14\frac{3}{8} \times 9\frac{1}{2}$ in. (36.5 × 24.1 cm).

French. *Woman's bonnet*, c. 1815.
Straw trimmed with silk plain weave (taffeta).

American. *Pair of sleeve puffers*, c. 1830.
Silk plain weave and down.

Probably English. *Stays*, c. 1825.
Cotton sateen, corded, bone eyelets.

American. *Dress*, c. 1825. Silk damask, silk gauze, silk bobbin lace, silk cord, linen lining.

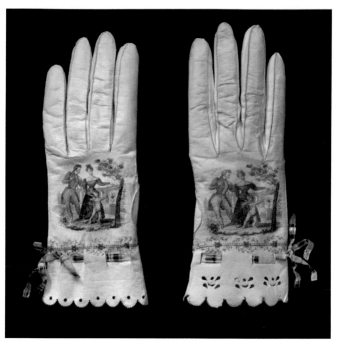

Spanish. *Pair of women's gloves*, c. 1830.
Kid leather, printed (intaglio) and painted, silk ribbon.

French. *Court dress*, c. 1830. Silk satin,
embroidered with metallic threads.

Petit Courrier des Dames.
Boulevard des Italiens N.º 2, près le passage de l'Opéra.

French. Plate 437 from *Petit Courrier des Dames*, 1824–29.
Etching with hand-applied color, 12½ × 9½ in. (31.8 × 24.1 cm).

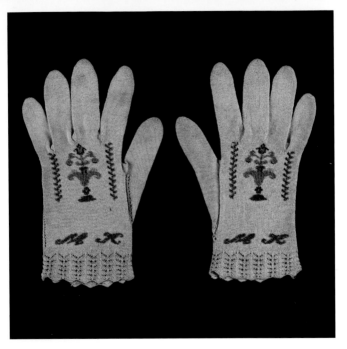

European. *Pair of women's gloves*, 1839.
Cotton knit and glass beads.

American. *Dress*, c. 1839.
Silk damask.

American. *Dress with matching cape*, 1839.
Silk damask, silk-covered buttons, cotton twill lining,
padding, metal boning, metal hook-and-eye closure.

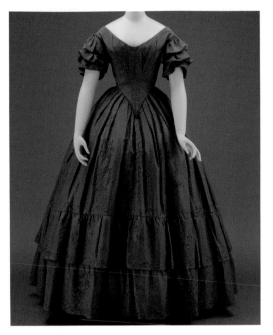

American (Boston). *Dinner dress*, c. 1840.
Silk plain weave (faille) with silk embroidery, glazed cotton
plain weave lining, cotton plain weave gauze sleeve lining,
cotton plain weave tape, baleen, metal hooks.

American. *Wedding dress*, c. 1840. Silk satin, cotton lining,
whalebone, metal hook-and-eye closures.

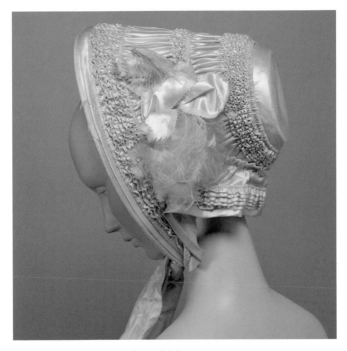

French. *Bride's bonnet*, c. 1840.
White satin and feathers.

MID-19TH CENTURY

1846–1870

By the mid-nineteenth century, women's skirts became so wide that the number of petticoats required to achieve fullness became cumbersome and a new solution was required: the cage crinoline or hoopskirt. Light-steel hoops connected by fabric tapes allowed skirts to be held out in a dome. In the interest of modesty—for hoops could easily be caught by the wind—pantalets or drawers began to be worn under ladies' dresses. The wide skirt also visually slimmed the waistline, which was accentuated by a corset and sometimes bust padding.

The production of aniline dyes, beginning in 1856, allowed textile manufactures to produce brilliant colors such as purple, bright green, and magenta. Elaborate ruffles, lace, artificial flowers, and ribbons reflected the prosperity of the period, particularly in Europe. The advent of department stores and sewing machines (patented in 1846) made fashionable garments more accessible to a wider clientele. This era also saw the beginning of haute couture: Charles Frederick Worth, an Englishman who began his career in the textile trade, founded the House of Worth in Paris in 1845. He was the designer of choice of the French Empress Eugenie, and dramatically changed the way that women purchased their clothing. Instead of a dressmaker making garments under the direction of a client, buyers visited Worth's salon to view his seasonal collections, making selections from them and putting themselves in the master's hands.

By 1865, the volume of skirts shifted to the back, anticipating the bustled styles of the 1870s. As the fullness of the skirt moved completely to the back, it was supported by the half-crinoline or crinolette, a petticoat that was straight at the front with hoops at the back, sometimes with horsehair-stiffened pads just under the waist for additional support of the looped-up skirt.

Fashionable men of the 1840s wore low, tightly cinched waists, with rounded chests and flared frock coats inspired by Prince Albert, husband of Queen Victoria. Trousers were tight and waistcoats had high upstanding collars worn with neckties tied around them. By the 1850s, men's styles became more relaxed with wider sleeves, higher waistlines, and longer, straight-cut jackets. Trousers became looser, with straight-cut legs or the "peg-top" which was cut more generously at the hips and tapered to the ankle. During the 1860s, trousers and jackets loosened further, and jackets extended to thigh length. Later in the decade the male silhouette slimmed down again, reflecting trends in the female silhouette. Technology had a profound effect on men's clothing, with shirts, underwear, accessories, and even trousers increasingly being made by machine.

American. *Cape*, 1850s. Silk plain weave (taffeta)
and net, with silk-velvet ribbon.

Worn by Georgiana Welles (Sargent), American, 1818–1879.
Woman's dress (two bodices, skirt, shawl), c. 1854. Silk plain weave (taffeta
moiré), trimmed with silk ribbon, silk machine net, bobbin lace.

Southworth and Hawes, American, active 1843–62.
"Martha Pickman Rogers in her wedding gown," 1850s.
Daguerreotype, 5¼ × 4 in. (13.3 × 10 cm).

American (Boston). Jones, Ball & Poor, 1846–1853. *Gem-set brooch with pendant drop*, c. 1850. Gold, diamond, pink topaz.

American. *Woman's dress and matching cape*, c. 1850.
Printed cotton plain weave, with supplementary weft patterning.

François Claudius Compte-Calix, French, 1813–1880.
Preparatory drawing for "Les Modes Parisiennes," 1856.
Watercolor and graphite on bristol board.

American. *Day dress*, c. 1855. Silk plain weave,
with weft float patterning silk fringe.

French, worn in America. *Woman's headdress*, mid-nineteenth century.
Wire, silk, gum arabic, starch, beeswax, pigments, glass, gelatin.

American or French. *Ball dress*, c. 1858. Silk plain weave (taffeta),
machine net (tulle), silk bobbin lace, trimmed with silk ribbon,
embroidered silk net, silk flowers.

French, for Champagne & Rougier, printed by Jacomme & Cie.
Print illustrating a design for a woman's woven silk skirt, 1850–55.
Lithograph with hand-applied color and pencil,
12¼ × 10⅝ in. (30.9 × 27 cm).

English, worn in America. *Pair of woman's slippers*, c. 1850.
Leather, silk plain weave (taffeta) and lace, machine embroidery, silk
satin, cotton plain weave, metal buckle (probably gold-plated brass).

William Morris Hunt, American, 1824–1879.
Mrs. Robert C. Winthrop (Frances Pickering Adams), 1861.
Oil on canvas, 46⅛ × 35¼ in. (117.16 × 89.53 cm).

Manufactured by Edmund Soper Hunt Fan Factory, American, late nineteenth century. *Fan*, 1867–70. Silk satin leaf, tape, pierced wood sticks covered with gold leaf, mother-of-pearl, brass.

Mme. Roger, French, active mid-nineteenth century.
Woman's evening dress, c. 1865. Silk plain weave (faille) and satin,
trimmed with silk satin ribbon, net, silk lace.

Mme. Roger, French, active mid-nineteenth century.
Woman's evening dress, c. 1868, restored about 1963. Silk plain
weave patterned with weft floats, net, satin and blond lace.

American. *Woman's dress*, c. 1865. Silk plain weave (taffeta),
silk satin, bobbin appliqué lace, silk-covered buttons,
linen lining, metal hook-and-eye closure.

European or American. *Crinoline*, c. 1870.
Cotton damask and steel.

Retailed by Tiffany & Co., American, active 1837–present.
The Colt family suite in three parts (necklace), 1856.
Gold, enamel, diamond.

American. *Day dress of piña cloth*, 1868–70.
Pineapple leaf fiber (piña) plain weave, silk plain weave
underdress trimmed with silk net.

LATE 19TH CENTURY
1870–1905

The late nineteenth-century, the Gilded Age in America and the Belle Epoque in Europe, was an era of extravagance and excess. Bustled styles continued to dominate the 1870s and 1880s, sometimes reaching nearly comical proportions. Women's figures were molded and shaped by steel-boned corsets, as well as padded and hooped bustles, to achieve an exaggerated version of the "ideal" female figure.

The cuirass bodice—named after joined breast and back-plates in armor—was a heavily boned, tight-fitting bodice. This bodice was longer than those of the 1860s and was worn over a skirt that looped up at the back. The polonaise bodice, an adaptation of eighteenth-century dress, extended from the waist to the knee and was worn with an underskirt. By the 1890s, the bustle had all but disappeared, and the fashionable silhouette was formed by the S-bend corset. Originally conceived as a health corset to take pressure off the abdomen, the S-bend thrust the bust forward and the hips back, creating a strong curve in the spine. Dresses in the 1890s featured ornate lace, beads, and ribbon. Sleeves were often very full, typically ending at the elbow for evening styles, or tightening from elbow to wrist for daytime, in leg-of-mutton style.

The MFA's collection is weighted toward evening styles, but society women of the era were expected to change their clothing as many as five times per day. Relatively simple morning or day dresses were replaced by tweeds and blouses, tea gowns, sportswear for activities such as cycling or croquet, and dinner dresses and balldresses. Each ensemble required accessories such as elaborate hats, veils, gloves, jewelry, stockings, handbags, and parasols.

The 1890s saw the beginnings of change in the roles of women in society. Women increasingly began to participate in outdoor activities, particularly cycling, which with the addition of the advent of train travel gave women more freedom of movement. The ideal young woman of the era was embodied in the Gibson Girl character featured in illustrations by Charles Dana Gibson from 1890 to 1910—a stylish, free-spirited woman with high-piled hair and fashionable curves.

In this era, the standard elements of menswear generally remained the same, becoming leaner in the 1880s and 1890s. The full-skirted frock coat and cutaway morning coat were worn for formal occasions and business. The sack suit featuring a looser jacket, often paired with a matching waistcoat and trousers, was also fashionable. Evening occasions called for the formal black tailcoat, a matching double-breasted waistcoat, starched white shirt and bow tie, and black trousers. In the 1880s, the tuxedo debuted, a formal version of the sack suit. The top hat was the most formal style of headwear for men; the bowler was worn with more causal looks.

Designed by Charles Frederick Worth, English (active in France),
c. 1825–1895, designed for House of Worth, French, 1858–1956.
Woman's dress, c. 1870. Silk plain weave (faille),
supplementary warp stripe pattern, lace.

French. *Parasol*, c. 1869.
Silk lace and ivory.

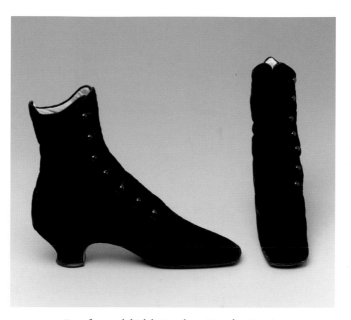

Pair of women's high button shoes, French, 1875–80.
Silk velvet, silk faille lining, glass buttons, leather.

Joseph Florentin Léon Bonnat, French, 1833–1922.
Mary Sears (later Mrs. Francis Shaw), 1878.
Oil on canvas, 49¾ × 29½ in. (126.4 × 75 cm).

Retailed by John J. Stevens, American.
Walking dress, 1874–75. Silk plain weave (faille) and silk fringe.

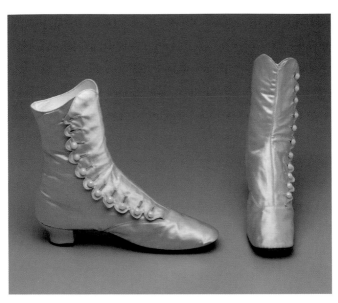

Made by T. E. Moseley & Co., American (Boston).
Pair of wedding shoes, 1877. Silk satin, linen plain weave,
leather, glass buttons.

European. *Natural pearl and diamond necklace*, c. 1880. Silver, gold, natural pearls *(pinctada maxima)*, diamonds.

Designed by Charles Frederick Worth, English (active in France),
c. 1825–1895, for House of Worth, French, 1858–1956. *Afternoon dress*,
c. 1880. Silk plain weave (faille), silk satin, and silk cut-and-uncut
velvet, trimmed with silk plain weave (chiffon) and silk fringe.

Designed by Charles Frederick Worth, English (active in France),
c. 1825–1895, for House of Worth, French, 1858–1956.
Dinner dress, c. 1883. Silk damask, satin, plain weave (taffeta), glass
beads, metallic yarn, with silk fringe and machine-made lace.

John Singer Sargent, American, 1856–1925.
Mrs. Edward Darley Boit (Mary Louisa Cushing), 1887.
Oil on canvas, 60 × 42¾ in. (152.4 × 108.58 cm).

Designed by Charles Frederick Worth, English (active in France),
c. 1825–1895, for House of Worth, French, 1858–1956. *Evening dress*,
c. 1888. Silk plain weave patterned with weft floats, trimmed with silk
plain weave (chiffon), satin ribbons, jet beads, machine net.

Emile Pingat, French, active 1860–1896. *Woman's coat*, c. 1883–90.
Silk velvet embroidered with silk,
silk lace, chenille fringe, feathers, silk braid.

Probably Italian. *Folding fan*, early twentieth century.
Feathers and synthetic sticks.

Retailed by Le Bon Marché department store, French, founded 1858.
Evening mantle, 1900. Silk velvet, silk plain weave (chiffon),
silk lace with jet and rhinestones.

Painted by A. Deluc, French, late nineteenth century.
Fan, 1883–85. Skin leaf painted in gouache; carved, painted,
and varnished mother-of-pearl sticks.

Possibly by Streeter & Co., Ltd., English. *Bicycle brooch*, mid-1890s.
Gold, enamel, diamond (old brilliant cuts), ruby.

American. *Corset: "The Cyclist, WB Special, Aug 25, 1895,"* c. 1895.
Silk satin, cotton twill, steel, elastic, trimmed with
silk lace and satin ribbon.

L. Perchellet, French. *Pair of women's shoes*, 1895.
Silk satin, leather, sequins, beads.

Marcus & Co., American, 1892–1941.
Necklace, c. 1900. Gold, peridot, diamond,
platinum, plique-à-jour enamel, pearl.

EARLY 20TH CENTURY
1906–1937

Fashion in the first decade of the twentieth century mainly continued the trends of the late nineteenth. The S-bend silhouette still dominated, accompanied by enormous hats to balance the top-heavy shape. The arrival of the Ballets Russes from St. Petersburg to Paris in 1909, with colorful sets and costumes designed by Léon Bakst, inspired new artistic experimentation that carried over into fashion. A new columnar silhouette emerged, led by the designer Paul Poiret.

The First World War (1914–1918) created social and economic conditions that altered fashion: women were required to join the workforce in place of men on the front lines, requiring more practical attire. In 1914, skirt shapes changed from the narrow, columnar "hobble" style to a bell shape, once again requiring multiple petticoats. Hemlines began to rise by 1916, and footwear became more of a focal point. In 1913, Gabrielle "Coco" Chanel opened her first dress shop, offering casual, sporty clothing in pared-down silhouettes that suited the war years. Chanel's designs would continue to be influential for many decades.

The 1920s were characterized by simplicity of line, introducing the *garçonne* look, a youthful, boyish style that differed dramatically from previous silhouettes. Hemlines rose and waistlines fell to the hip. The characteristic simplicity of the *garçonne* look did not extend to fabrics and embellishment; evening wear was often heavily decorated with beadwork, sequins, and embroidery. The iconic close-fitting cloche hat required short hair, and by 1926 short haircuts were the norm for stylish women.

The ideal of a slender figure persisted in the 1930s, but hemlines descended and the waistline returned to its natural position. The bias cut, perfected by designer Madeleine Vionnet, became a popular way to highlight feminine curves. The Great Depression of the 1930s coincided with the advent of the movie star, whose very existence depended on projecting an image of glamour. Day looks included impeccably tailored skirt suits and feminine dresses in floral, dotted, and abstract prints, while evening wear featured long, body-skimming lines, shoulder-baring straps, and low-cut backs.

In the 1910s, men increasingly adopted the three-piece lounge suit—consisting of a sack coat, waistcoat, and trousers—a casual alternative to the formal suits of previous years. Trousers rose to ankle length, often with turned-up cuffs, and starched collars were worn high on the neck. As with womenswear, the 1920s and 1930s saw greater simplicity in men's styles. Collars became softer and one- or two-button jackets of tweed or flannel were popular. For formal events, dark tailcoats worn with a waistcoat and trousers gave way to the less formal tuxedo.

Designed by John Redfern, English, 1853–1929,
for House of Redfern, French (Paris). *Evening dress*, c. 1905.
Silk plain weave (taffeta and chiffon), lamé, and silk net
embroidered with metallic thread and beads.

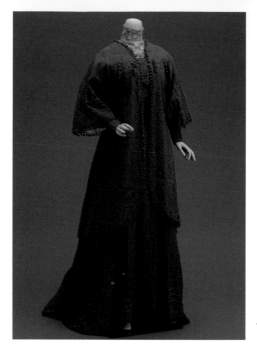

American. *Woman's day dress (with coat)*, c. 1906.
Wool twill (broadcloth), silk twill,
soutache braid, silk tassels, boning.

American. *Woman's day dress (without coat)*, c. 1906.

Cheri-Rousseau and Glauth, French,
late nineteenth–early twentieth centuries. *Woman and Mirror*, c. 1910.
Gelatin silver print, 7 × 11 in. (17.8 × 27.9 cm).

Miss Brady, Miss McCormack, American (Boston). *Hat*, c. 1910.
Plaited straw with silk velvet ribbon and silk flowers.

LA QUESTION EST POSEE : portera-t-on la jupe-pantalon en 1911 ??

15 — Cette mode mal accueillie à la Comédie-Française, fait la joie des habitués des Courses d'Auteuil. Dans les grands ateliers de couture on rivalise d'ingéniosité pour la rendre élégante et commode. ND Phot.

Published by Neurdein et Cie., Paris, France, c. 1860s–1919.
La Question est Posee: portera-t-on la Jupe-Pantalon en 1911??
Gelatin silver print, 5½ × 3½ in. (14 × 8.9 cm).

Designed by Brooks, American (Philadelphia). *Woman's suit*, c. 1910.
Wool twill, silk braid, silk plain weave, metal, plastic, linen lace,
cotton plain weave, cotton embroidery.   157

Retailed by Smith Importer, American (Springfield, MA).
Hat, probably French, c. 1910–15.
Plaited straw and feathers.

Designed by Kater and Brooks, American (Philadelphia).
Woman's suit, c. 1910. Silk and linen plain weave, silk plain weave with
supplementary weft float patterning, metal, mother-of-pearl. 159

Liberty & Co., English, founded 1875.
Woman's evening coat, 1915–20.
Silk satin embroidered with silk.

John Paul Cooper, English, 1869–1933.
Brooch, 1908. Gold (15K), abalone, tourmaline, moonstone,
pearl, amethyst, chrysoprase, jade(?).

Robe de plage en foulard garni de tussor gros grain chapeau en Suède rouge

George Barbier, French, 1882–1932. *"Robe de plage en foulard garni de tussor gros grain chapeau en Suède rouge,"* plate 15 from *Journal des Dames et des Modes,* 1912. Etching with hand-applied color (pochoir), 9 × 5½ in. (22.9 × 14 cm).

Designed by Jeanne Lanvin, French, 1867–1946,
for House of Lanvin, French, founded 1889.
Woman's dress, c. 1914. Silk plain weave (taffeta),
net, silk velvet ribbons, silk flowers.

Labeled Puddington, designed by Ella M. Puddington,
American. *Woman's coat*, 1910–20. Jacquard-woven wool, silk velvet,
silk cording, soda glass buttons, silk satin lining.

Retailed by R. H. Stearns & Co, American.
Hat, c. 1914. Silk velvet, fur, ostrich feather.

House of Premet, French, 1911–1931.
Evening dress, c. 1914. Silk satin, silk plain weave (chiffon),
moiré, net, trimmed with net and silk flowers.

W. C. Keen, American (Boston).
Hat, c. 1915. Plaited straw and feathers.

Maison Agnès, French, 1898–1952.
Woman's evening dress, c. 1914. Silk plain weave (chiffon),
silver lamé, net and lace, embroidered and appliquéd with taffeta,
metallic thread, rhinestones, glass beads.

Edward Everett Oakes, American, 1891–1960.
Circular brooch, c. 1920. Gold, diamond, sapphire.

Minnis and Simons, American (Boston).
Woman's hat, 1915–20.
Silk plain weave (taffeta), straw, braid, feathers.

Designed by Maurice Babani, French, for Babani, French, founded 1895. *Woman's tea gown*, c. 1919–30. Silk velvet, embroidered with metallic thread and silk-and-metallic cord, silk plain weave lining.

172

Probably American. *Woman's tea gown*, 1910–20.
Silk velvet, batik-dyed.

Mariano Fortuny (y Madrazo), Spanish, 1871–1949.
"Delphos" dress and belt, c. 1937.
Pleated silk satin and glass beads.

Mariano Fortuny (y Madrazo), Spanish, 1871–1949.
Tea gown, c. 1920. Silk velvet stenciled with gold and silver
pigment, silk plain weave, pleated, glass beads.

Possibly French or American. *Pair of shoes*, 1925–30.
Silk satin with gold-metallic patterning wefts and leather,
gold metallic buckle with rhinestones.

Probably French. *Feather brisé fan*, 1915–25.
Dyed feathers; reformed protein sticks and guards.

Probably American. *Hat*, c. 1920.
Silk satin and feathers.

American. *Handbag*, 1920s.
Metal, lacquer, silk.

Fabric by H. R. Mallinson and Company, American, 1915–36,
fabric designed by Walter Mitschke, American (born in Germany),
180   1886–1972. *Woman's hat*, 1929. Printed silk, plain weave, quilted.

Fabric by H. R. Mallinson and Company, American, 1915–36, fabric designed by Walter Mitschke, American (born in Germany), 1886–1972. *Dress*, c. 1927. Silk plain weave, printed.

181

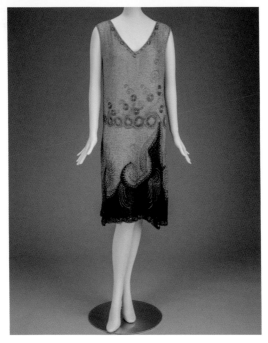

Probably French. *Woman's dress*, c. 1925.
Cotton plain weave and embroidered with glass beads.

Attributed to Gabrielle "Coco" Chanel, French, 1883–1971,
Dress, French (Paris), c. 1926. Silk velvet embroidered
with metallic thread, glass beads, paillettes.

Edward Steichen, American, 1879–1973.
Marian Morehouse for *Vogue*, May 1, 1927.
Gelatin silver print, 9⅞ × 7⅞ in. (25.1 × 20 cm).

Designed by Madeleine Chéruit, French, d. 1935,
for House of Chéruit, French, 1906–1935. *Woman's dress*, 1927.
Silk plain weave (chiffon) and sequins.

Jantzen, British. *Woman's swimsuit*, American, 1925–29.
Wool, cotton, latex rubber knit ("Lastex"),
jacquard-woven cotton.

Jantzen, British. *Man's swimsuit*, American, 1930–35.
Wool, cotton, latex rubber knit ("Lastex"),
metal zipper and buckle.

Designed by Juliette Moutard, French, for René Boivin,
French, founded 1890, fabricated by Charles Profilet, French,
worn by Claudette Colbert, American (born in France), 1903–1996.
Starfish brooch, 1937. Gold (18K), ruby, amethyst.

Designed by Main Rousseau Bocher, known as Mainbocher,
American (active France), 1891–1976. *Evening dress*, 1930s.
Silk plain weave (charmeuse) and lamé.

Elmer Fryer, American, 1898–1944.
Dolores del Rio for "in Caliente," 1930–40.
Gelatin silver print, 10 × 8 in. (25.4 × 20.3 cm).

Designed by Jeanne Lanvin, French, 1867–1946, for House of Lanvin, French, founded 1889. *Woman's evening ensemble*, Winter 1935–36. Silk plain-weave (crepe), trimmed with gilt leather.

Marcel Rochas, French, 1902–1959. *Woman's ensemble in three parts (jacket, blouse, skirt)*, Fall 1935. Silk plain weave, printed (chiné), silk velvet, plastic buttons, metal snaps and hooks..

American. *Pair of woman's shoes*, 1930s. Leather.

MID-20TH CENTURY
1938–1960

World War Two (1939–1945) had a strong impact on fashion. Most Paris design houses were shut down, and contact with Europe was difficult. Clothing rationing led to a simpler, severe aesthetic, especially in Great Britain where styles featured nipped-in waistlines, padded shoulders, and hems just below the knee. In the United States, distance from Paris led to the development of a stronger American fashion industry. Claire McCardell created simple, sporty pieces using materials such as cotton denim, jersey, and seersucker when wool and silk became sparse. Norman Norell used unrationed sequins to create shimmering sheath dresses that added glamour to the bleak war years.

In the postwar period, Paris returned to dominance as the world's fashion capital. Christian Dior introduced the New Look in 1947, reviving the hourglass shape of earlier eras, and including a long, full skirt, in contrast to the less extravagant use of fabric required by wartime rationing. The 1950s saw a return to more defined gender roles, as illustrated by the formal, overtly feminine styles available for women. The decade also witnessed the emergence of multiple stylish silhouettes introduced by designers such as Charles James, Cristóbal Balenciaga, and Hubert de Givenchy. The nipped-in waist and full-skirted styles and straighter-cut suits and sheath dresses were considered equally stylish. The craze for sportswear grew during this period, with the introduction of twinsets and pedal pushers, as well as sundresses and swimsuits. The 1950s also saw the introduction of the cocktail dress, which combined the length of day wear with the embellishment of evening wear.

Men's fashion of this era moved toward informality, in contrast to the elegance of women's styles. Young men led the new rebellious "youth culture" and looked to actors such as James Dean and Marlon Brando for styles adapted from the working class. In Great Britain, the working class Teddy Boys adopted the velvet-collared jacket and narrow trousers of the Savile Row New Edwardian style originally worn by upper-class men. More generally, men's suits were baggy in shape, and in the 1950s, more color was introduced through shirts or ties and cummerbunds worn with tuxedos.

Star Millinery Shop, American. *Hat*, 1938–42.
Plaited straw, net, ribbon, synthetic fruit.

Designed by Travis Banton, American, 1894–1958,
worn by Anna May Wong, Chinese American, 1905–1961.
Woman's evening dress, 1934. Silk satin, embroidered.

Howard Greer, American, 1896–1974.
Women's evening dress, 1940s. Silk plain weave and gauze,
rayon plain weave and bugle beads.

Koret, American, founded 1929. *Handbag*, 1940s.
Gilt leather on suede.

Drécoll, French (Paris). *Dress*, 1936.
Silk plain weave (crepe) with silk satin ribbon.

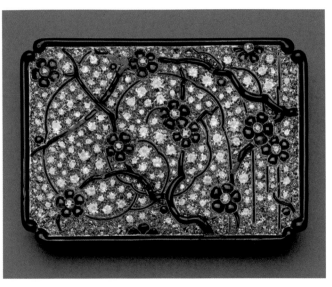

Lacloche Frères, Spanish, founded 1875 (also worked in Paris).
Japanesque brooch, c. 1925. Platinum, gold,
enamel, diamond, ruby, onyx.

Elsa Schiaparelli, Italian (active in France), 1890–1973,
fabric by Ducharne, French, founded 1920. *Evening dress*,
Summer 1939. Silk twill and silk plain weave (moiré).

Designed by Norman Hartnell, English, 1901–1979,
retailed by Berketex. *Woman's "Utility" dress*, c. 1942.
Wool plain weave, fulled.

Fashion Sport, English. Labeled CC41,
English, 1941–52. *Woman's skirt and blouse*, c. 1945.
Linen plain weave, printed.

Mackey Starr, American (New York).
Pair of woman's shoes, 1940s. Suede and leather.

American. *Woman's suit,* 1940s.
Wool twill.

Gilbert Adrian, American, 1903–1959.
Woman's dress: Love and Tears, 1943.
208   Silk plain weave (crepe), printed.

Gilbert Adrian, American, 1903–1959.
Woman's dress: Roan Stallion, 1943.
Silk plain weave (crepe), printed.

209

American. *Bejeweled gloves*, 1940s.
Suede, plastic, metal.

American. *Handbag*, 1940s.
Suede, plastic, metal.

Designed by Elizabeth Hawes, American, 1903–1971.
Dinner dress, 1935–37. Silk satin.

Elizabeth Arden, American, founded 1910.
Woman's lounge dress, early 1940s.
Silk satin, cotton, Lurex belt.

Cristóbal Balenciaga, Spanish (active in France), 1895–1972.
"Matador" ensemble, c. 1948, restyled in the 1950s. Silk and velvet;
214   embroidered with metallic thread and silk fringe.

House of Balenciaga, French (Paris).
Hat, 1950s. Silk satin trimmed
with silk passementerie and jet.

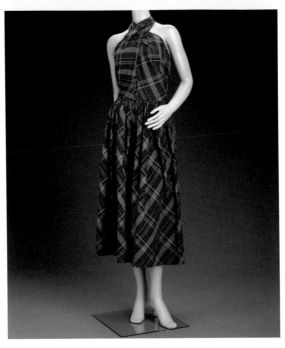

Designed by Claire McCardell, American, 1905–1958,
for Townley. *Woman's dress*, c. 1950. Cotton plain weave
and brass hook-and-eye closures.

American. *Philadelphia hinge bracelet*, c. 1935.
Plastic (phenolic resin) and metal.

Carolyn Schnurer, American, 1908–1998.
Sun suit, 1945–55. Cotton plain weave, printed.

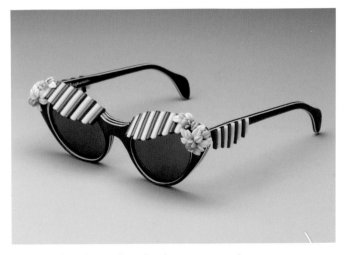

Elsa Schiaparelli, Italian (active in France), 1890–1973,
manufactured by American Optical. *Sunglasses*, 1950s.
Plastic and glass lenses.

Charles James, American (born in England), 1906–1978.
Evening dress, 1951.
Silk plain weave (chiffon) and satin.

Charles James, American (born in England), 1906–1978.
Evening dress, 1950.
Silk satin and plain weave (taffeta).

Designed by Roger Vivier, French, 1908–1998, designed for House of
Christian Dior, French, founded 1946. *Pair of women's pumps*, 1957–58.
Silk satin with metal clip; leather sole and lining.

Jan Leslie, American (New York).
Woman's hat, 1959–60. Wool felt and feathers.

Designed by Christian Dior, French, 1905–1957,
for House of Christian Dior, French, founded 1946.
Cocktail ensemble, Autumn/Winter 1955. Silk satin, printed.

James Galanos, American, b. 1924.
Woman's dress, 1950s.
Warp printed silk plain weave (taffeta).

Designed by Gabrielle "Coco" Chanel, French, 1883–1971, designed
for House of Chanel, French, founded 1909. *Woman's day suit*, 1955–60.
Wool twill and printed cotton plain weave.

Adolpho II. *Hat*, c. 1955. Wool felt.

William Klein, American, b. 1928. *Smoke and Veil*, 1958.
Gelatin silver print, 19⅞ × 15⅞ in. (50.5 × 40.3 cm).

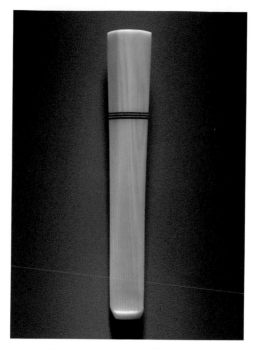

American. *Cigarette holder*, c. 1955.
Plastic, white metal, pigment.

Arnold Scaasi, American, 1930–2015, worn by Arlene Francis,
American, 1907–2001. *Evening dress and coat*, 1958.
Silk and silver metallic thread matelassé and silk satin.

Arnold Scaasi, American, 1930–2015.
Woman's cocktail dress and coat, 1958. Silk plain weave,
printed; silk satin weave, silk net.

LATE 20TH CENTURY
1968–1999

Women's fashion of the 1960s followed three main trajectories: the continued feminine elegance of the 1950s; youthful, innovative styles influenced by space exploration; and the late 1960s bohemian hippie style. While designers such as Balenciaga continued to produce ladylike straight-cut suits and beautifully constructed dresses, innovators like Mary Quant created the iconic miniskirt, using new materials such as acrylic, polyester, and PVC. The later years of the decade saw the appearance of hippie styles inspired by non-Western cultures and Art Nouveau. Both the "mod" look of Mary Quant and later hippie looks appealed to the post-WWII "baby boomers" who defined the culture of the era.

By the middle of the 1970s, designers were looking to the 1930s and 1940s for inspiration, incorporating longer, figure-hugging silhouettes. The disco and glam rock trends later in the decade inspired Halston and Arnold Scassi, whose designs featured sequins, velvet, and feathers. The consumerist 1980s era was personified by the young urban professional, or "yuppie." Heavily padded shoulders and power suits were common for women, while "designer" fashion, often festooned with logos, was worn to signal wealth and status. The new opulence brought about a revival of the Paris couturiers after the youth-lead movements of the 1960s and 1970s. Western fashion also became more international, and Japanese designers beginning with Issey Miyake in the early 70s, and later Yohji Yamamato and Rei Kawakubo, emerged and introduced cutting-edge designs that featured innovative fabric and draping.

The 1990s saw a resurgence of street style and subcultures influencing high fashion. In the early 1990s, grunge, a mixture of punk and hippie aesthetics popularized by the Seattle, WA, music scene, was reinterpreted by a number of designers. Vivienne Westwood, who had helped lead the punk movement of the late 1970s, turned to historical dress to create new looks.

Menswear of the 1960s changed dramatically for the first time in decades, becoming more casual and colorful. By the late 1960s, many men were wearing bold prints and Eastern-influenced styles such as the Nehru jacket. In the 1970s, the fashionable men's silhouette was tall and slim. Suits were available in a wide range of colors and fabrics, and a less formal version of the suit made in light fabrics and pale colors, known as the leisure suit, also appeared. Toward the end of the decade, the silhouette widened again, with double-breasted jackets and wider shoulders a precursor to the ubiquitous padded shoulders of 1980s power dressing. The 1990s were more dressed down for men, with single-breasted suits with softer shoulders and Nehru-style jackets again becoming fashionable.

Arnold Scaasi, American, 1930–2015.
Woman's ensemble worn by Dame Joan Sutherland, 1963. Silk satin weave,
silk plain weave, voided velvet, tulle, linen plain weave.

Cristóbal Balenciaga, Spanish (active in France), 1895–1972.
Woman's evening dress, Spring–Summer 1961.
Warp-printed silk plain weave (taffeta chiné).

Jean Dessès, French (born in Egypt), 1904–1970.
Woman's evening dress, c. 1960.
Silk plain weave (chiffon).

Arnold Scaasi, American, 1930–2015.
Woman's dress, Fall 1961. Silk plain weave (chiffon).

Arnold Scaasi, American, 1930–2015.
Sketch book – Fall 1961, 1961. Ink, pencil, or paint on paper
and silk chiffon, 11 × 9 in. (28 × 23 cm).

Designed by Flirtette Creation, American.
Woman's hat, 1960s. Plastic braid, cotton velvet,
synthetic net (foundation).

William Klein, American, b. 1928.
Simone & Nina, Piazza di Spagna, Rome (Vogue), 1960 (printed later).
Gelatin silver print, 19¾ × 15⅞ in. (50.4 × 40.4 cm).

HIRO, Japanese American, b. 1930.
Alberta Tiburzi, New York, October 28, 1966, printed in 2001.
Chromogenic print, 22 × 15 in. (55.9 × 38.1 cm).

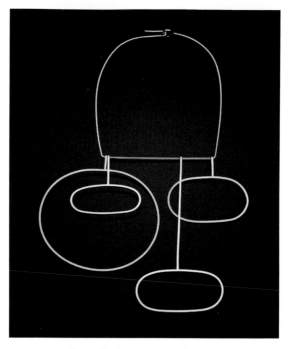

Betty Cooke, American, b. 1924.
Necklace, c. 1959. Silver.

Designed by Cristóbal Balenciaga, Spanish (active France), 1895–1972, fabric by Lemarié, French, founded 1880. *Woman's dress*, Autumn/Winter 1966. Silk plain weave and ostrich feathers.

Designed by Annika Rimala, Finnish, b. 1936, for Marimekko, Finnish,
founded 1951. Retailed by Design Research, American, 1953–78.
Woman's raincoat ensemble (coat and head scarf), 1960s. Coated,
screen-printed cotton plain weave (oilcloth).

Distributed by Campbell Soup Company, American, founded 1960s.
Woman's paper "Souper Dress," c. 1967.
Cellulose and cotton nonwoven fabric, printed.

Designed by Emilio Pucci, Inc., Italian, founded c. 1948.
Woman's ensemble, 1967. Silk plain weave (chiffon), screen printed.

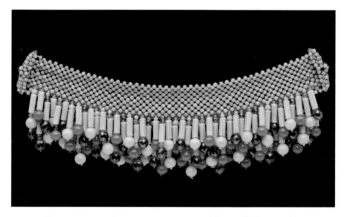

Coppola e Toppo, Italian, 1940–1986, possibly made for Emilio Pucci, Italian, 1914–1992. *Beaded choker*, 1960–69. Brass and glass.

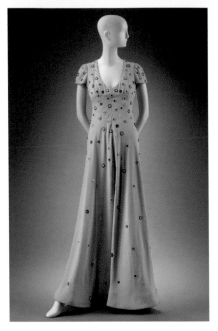

Arnold Scaasi, American, 1930–2015.
Dress worn by Barbra Streisand to 1969 Oscars, 1970.
Synthetic plain weave (crepe) embroidered with metallic thread,
sequins, plastic beads, rhinestones.

Arnold Scaasi, American, 1930–2015.
Pants ensemble worn by Barbra Streisand to the 1968 Oscars, 1969.
Cotton plain weave, silk satin weave, silk tulle embroidered
with sequins, silk plain weave, metal.

Thea Porter, English (born in Jerusalem), 1927–2000.
Woman's coat, c. 1969. Wool embroidered with wool yarn,
trimmed with mink, lined with silk satin.

Designed by Thea Porter, English (born in Jerusalem), 1927–2000, retailed by Giorgio Beverly Hills. *Woman's caftan*, English (London), c. 1969. Silk plain weave (chiffon), resist dyed and embroidered with sequins, silk plain weave with discontinuous patterning wefts.

Retailed by Granny Takes a Trip (active 1966–74),
English, made by Gohill, English.
Pair of woman's boots, 1969. Appliquéd leather.

Thea Porter, English (born in Jerusalem), 1927–2000.
Woman's dress, c. 1970. Printed silk plain weave (chiffon), rayon and cotton damask, rayon velvet ribbon, lined with silk plain weave.

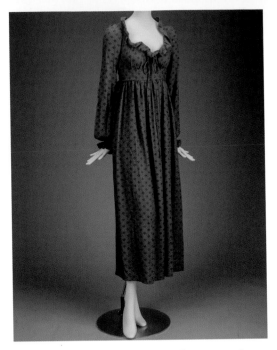

English. Labeled Biba, London, active late 1960s and 1970s.
Woman's dress, 1968–73. Wool twill, printed.

Biba, London, active late 1960s and 1970s, photographer
Sarah Moon, French, b. 1941. *Biba Archive: Skinny panne velvet
peplum suit*, 1974. Paper, 23 × 15⅛ in. (58.4 × 38.4 cm).

Designed by Ossie Clark, English, 1942–1996.
Woman's dress, early 1970s. Acetate and
rayon plain weave (crepe).

Designed by Yuki (Gnyuki Torimaru),
Japanese (active in England), b. 1937. *Woman's dress*, 1976.
Silk (microscopic fiber).

English. *Pair of woman's platform shoes*, 1970s.
Cotton velvet and silver.

Designed by Ossie Clark, English, 1942–1996.
"The Traffic Light Dress," 1970s. Rayon broken twill (crepe).

Designed by Azzedine Alaïa,
Tunisian (active Paris), 1935–2017. *Woman's dress*, c. 1986.
Wool knit and brass zippers.

Patrick Kelly, American, 1954–90.
Dress, 1986.
Wool knit embroidered with buttons.

Designed by Yuki (Gnyuki Torimaru), Japanese
(active in England), b. 1937. *Copy of dress worn by Diana Spencer,*
Princess of Wales, in 1986, 1997. Silk plain weave, pleated.

Designed by Yuki (Gnyuki Torimaru), Japanese (active in England), b. 1937. *Yuki sketch of blue Princess Diana dress*, 1986. Pigment on paper, 16½ × 11¾ in. (41.9 × 29.7 cm).

Designed by Christian Lacroix, French, born in 1951,
for House of Patou, French, founded 1914. *"Colin Maillard"
ensemble*, Spring 1987. Silk plain weave embroidered, silk lace,
tulle, silk satin; straw hat with silk flowers.

Designed by Christian Lacroix, French, born in 1951,
for House of Patou, French, founded 1914. *"Barbade"
evening ensemble*, Spring 1987. Silk plain weave, printed.

Herb Ritts, American, 1952–2002.
Wrapped Torso, Los Angeles, 1989.
Platinum print, 18¼ × 15⅛ in. (46.4 × 38.4 cm).

Designed by Issey Miyake, Japanese, b. 1938. *Dress: Hello Pleats*,
ISSEY MIYAKE Spring/Summer 1991.
Polyester, pleated using heat press.

Arnold Scaasi, American, 1930–2015.
Woman's evening dress, Fall 1989. Silk velvet, silk embroidery,
silk satin weave, silk plain weave, tulle, metal, plastic.

Vivienne Westwood, English, b. 1941.
Woman's dress, Fall/Winter 1991–92.
Viscose, Lycra®, foil, screen-printed.

Possibly American. *Clear Lucite box purse with large blue Lucite closure,*
mid–late twentieth century. Lucite set with rhinestones.

Designed by Isaac Mizrahi, American, b. 1961.
Horizon Blue Dress, Fall 1994. Wool (mohair) plain weave
and silk satin, embroidered with sequins.

Designed by Rei Kawakubo, Japanese, b. 1942, designed for Comme des Garçons, Ltd., Japanese, founded 1969. *Cardigan sweater and mixed plaid skirt*, Autumn/Winter 1993–94. Wool and nylon knit, cotton knit (jersey), fulled-wool twill, rayon plain weave, acrylic knit.

Designed by Rei Kawakubo, Japanese, b. 1942, designed for Comme des Garçons, Ltd., Japanese, founded 1969. *Coat dress, skirt, shoes*, Autumn/Winter 1996–97. Polyester and rayon voided velvet, cotton plain weave (muslin), polyester batting, leather, elastic, rubber.

Herb Ritts, American, 1952–2002.
Versace Dress, Back View, El Mirage, 1990.
Gelatin silver print, 54 × 43 in. (137.2 × 109.2 cm).

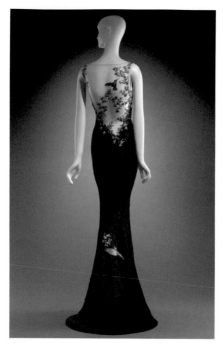

John Galliano, British (born in Gibraltar in 1960; works in Paris).
Dress worn by Cate Blanchett to 1998 Oscars, 1999.
Silk knit, silk embroidery, tulle, plastic.

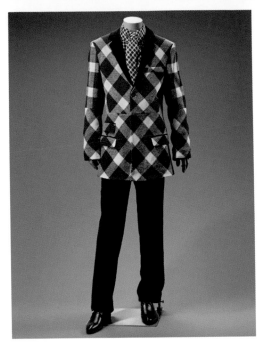

Vivienne Westwood, English, b. 1941.
Man's suit, shirt, and tie, 1990s.
Wool twill and cotton velvet.

Vivienne Westwood, English, b. 1941.
Dress with wrap, 1990s. Silk and synthetic plain weave
(seersucker) and synthetic net.

21ST CENTURY

2000–PRESENT

A return to an emphasis on luxury and consumption with a greater focus on self-expression characterized the early 2000s, as seen in the iconic television series *Sex and the City*, which featured four female characters each possessing an individual, but high-fashion, style. The show set, or reflected, many trends, including a mania for stiletto shoes by designers Manolo Blahnik and having the "it" handbag to demonstrate status and fashion sense.

In the early years of the twenty-first century, designers such as John Galliano and Alexander McQueen looked to global and historical references, but innovation and technology were the key trends and influences in the 2000s. McQueen and other designers employed digital printing to create new treatments for textiles, while designers like Iris van Herpen have used 3D printing to produce entire garments and shoes. Many designers are experimenting with techniques and materials while giving more consideration than ever before to issues of environmental sustainability and ethical manufacturing practices. Vivienne Westwood and Stella McCartney are both strong advocates for sustainable environmental and animal protection practices. McCartney uses materials such as re-engineered cashmere, organic cotton, and vegetarian "leather" to produce clothing with less detrimental impact on the environment.

While other eras have explored gender identity and dynamics, with women adopting menswear styles in the 1970s and 1980s to express power and independence, or men embracing colorful floral prints in the rebellious 1960s, issues of gender expression have moved to the forefront in the twenty-first century. For the millennial and younger generations, gender fluidity is the norm, and designers such as Walter van Beirendonck, and Rad Hourani—the first to present a unisex haute couture collection—challenge assumptions relating to gender in their designs.

The MFA continues to look to the future of fashion, collecting contemporary and emerging designers who are creating innovative, beautiful designs that demonstrate the artistry of fashion.

Manolo Blahnik, Spanish (active in England), b. 1942.
Women's shoes: Campari, 2007.
Patent leather.

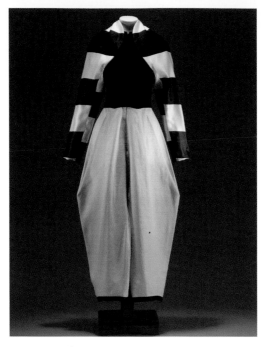

Geoffrey Beene, American, 1927–2004.
Jumpsuit and bolero, Spring 1993. Rayon knit (jersey),
linen plain weave, silk double-faced satin.

Geoffrey Beene, American, 1927–2004.
Woman's evening dress, Spring 2001.
Silk knit (jersey) and linen plain weave.

Designed by Helmut Lang, Austrian, b. 1956.
Woman's ensemble, made in Italy, Autumn/Winter, 2003–4.
Wool knit, plastic, elastic, cotton knit.

Designed by Helmut Lang, Austrian, b. 1956.
Man's ensemble, made in Italy, Spring/Summer 2004.
Elastic and synthetic knit, cotton double knit, leather, silver foil.   287

Karl Lagerfeld, German (active in France), 1933–2019, designed for House of Chanel, French, founded 1909, embroidered by Hurel, French, founded 1879. *Woman's evening dress*, Fall/Winter 2005. Silk satin, silk plain weave, embroidered with sequins and ostrich and cock feathers.

Karl Lagerfeld, German (active in France), 1933–2019, designed for House of Chanel, French, founded 1909. *Dress and coat*, Fall/Winter 2005. Silk satin weave, silk plain weave, sequins, ostrich and red junglefowl feathers, wool basketweave, glass beads. 289

Judith Leiber, American (born in Hungary), 1921–2018.
Crystal encrusted bird evening purse, c. 2000.
White metal and rhinestones.

Philip Treacy, Irish, b. 1967.
Hat, early twenty-first century.
Bukram, synthetic, plastic, glass.

Designed by Jean Paul Gaultier, French, b. 1952, ornaments
by Mariko Kusumoto, b. 1967. *Big in Japan ensemble*,
Spring/Summer 2019. Silk organza, pleated, silk damask,
silk plain weave, molded silk ornaments.

Designed by John Galliano, British (born in Gibraltar in 1960; works in Paris), for House of Christian Dior, French, founded 1946. *Woman's evening dress: Katisha-San*, Spring–Summer 2007. Silk satin and plain weave (faille) embroidered with silk and crystals.

Maison Martin Margiela, Belgian, founded 1989,
for Maison Martin Margiela Artisanal Collection. *Dress*, 2007.
294   Oil painting on cotton or linen canvas and silk under bodice.

Maison Martin Margiela, Belgian, founded 1989. *Semi Couture dressmaker's bodice and accessory*, Spring 1997. Linen plain weave, printed (bodice); silk chiffon plain weave and elastic (accessory).

House of Chanel, French, founded 1909.
Light bulb shoes, 2008.
Synthetic velvet, wood, metal, light bulbs.

Azzedine Alaïa, Tunisian (active in Paris), 1935–2017.
Woman's ensemble, Fall/Winter 2006.
Wool twill, cotton knit, goat hair.

Designed by Alexander McQueen CBE, English, 1969–2010.
Dress, Fall 2010. Silk jacquard, digitally printed.

Designed by Alexander McQueen CBE, English, 1969–2010.
Dress, Spring/Summer 2010. Silk plain weave, digitally printed;
embroidered with enamel plaques.

Issey Miyake, Japanese, b. 1938. *No. 1 dress, 132.5,*
ISSEY MIYAKE, 2010. Recycled polyester fabric,
folded using heat press with foil print.

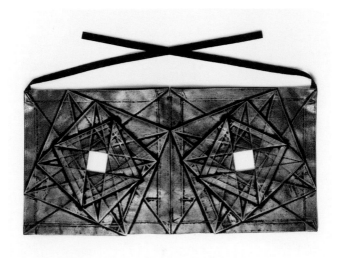

Issey Miyake, Japanese, b.1938 and Reality Lab. *Bolero, 132.5,*
ISSEY MIYAKE, 2010. Recycled polyester fabric,
folded using heat press with foil print.

Isabel Toledo, American (born in Cuba), 1961–2019.
"Wave" dress, 2011. Silk plain weave (taffeta).

Rodarte, American, founded 2005.
Dress, 2011. Silk plain weave (chiffon)
printed, machine-embroidered net.

Designed by Rodarte and Nicholas Kirkwood, English
(born in Germany), b. 1980, for Rodarte, American, founded 2005.
Pair of woman's shoes, 2011. Plastic, resin, elastic.

Designed by Oscar de la Renta, American (born in the Dominican Republic), 1932–2014. *Evening dress*, Pre-Fall 2010. Synthetic net, ombré dyed, embroidered with chiffon ribbon, sequins, beads.

Comme des Garçons, Ltd., Japanese, founded 1969.
Man's jacket and skirt, 2012 (jacket) and 1990 (skirt).
Wool plain weave and synthetic jacquard, printed.

Proenza Schouler, American, founded 2002. *Protest dress*,
Spring/Summer 2013. Double-faced silk satin, digitally printed;
308 embellished with silicone-coated nail heads and metal grommets.

Designed by Albert Kriemler, Swiss, b. 1960, for Akris, Swiss, founded 1922, after Geta Bratescu, Romanian, 1926–2018. *"Magnets in the City" Dress*, Swiss, 2019. Polyester plain weave, digitally printed. 309

Minju Kim, South Korea. *Pair of Shoes*, 2013.
Leather, metal, rubber.

Designed by Carla Fernandez, Mexican, b. 1973,
carved by Juan Alonso, Mexican. *Molinillo Shoes* (pair),
Summer 2013. Leather and wood.

Designed by Raf Simons, Belgian, b. 1968,
designed for House of Christian Dior, French, founded 1946.
Boots, 2013. Silk satin, embroidered with silk, beads.

Designed by Raf Simons, Belgian, b. 1968, designed for House of
Christian Dior, French, founded 1946. *Dress*, Autumn/Winter 2013.
Silk plain weave (chiffon), beaded and embroidered.

Designed by Iris van Herpen, Dutch, b. 1984,
for United Nude, established 2013. *Pair of shoes*, 2014.
Kid leather, metallicized.

Designed by Iris van Herpen, Dutch, b. 1984, designed by Neri Oxman, Israeli, b. 1976, printed by Stratasys. *Anthazoa 3D Cape and Skirt, Voltage Collection*, 2013. 3D-printed polyurethane rubber and acrylic, steel cage, cotton twill inner lining, silk satin lining. 315

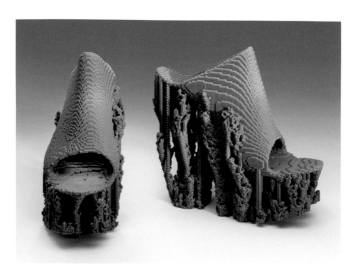

Designed by Francis Bitonti Studio Inc., American, b. 1983, printed
with Adobe Photoshop ©, printed by Fathom, Inc., American,
Oakland, CA. *Pair of "Molecule" Shoes*, 2015. 3D printed with Stratasys
Connex 3D Printer, printing software by Adobe Photoshop ©.

United Nude, established 2013.
Pair of Highrise Shoes, 2015. 3D printed, synthetic.

Designed by Rei Kawakubo, Japanese, b. 1942, designed for
Commes des Garçons, Ltd., Japanese, founded 1969. *Woman's dress*,
318   Autumn/Winter 2015–16. Cotton plain weave and nylon net.

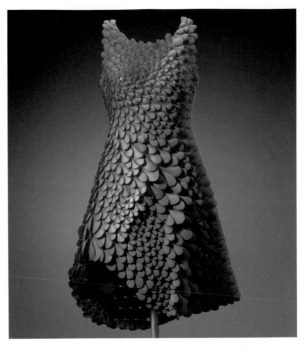

Jessica Rosenkrantz, American, b. 1983, Jesse Louis-Rosenberg, American, b. 1985, for Nervous System, established 2007. *Dress*, 2016. Laser-sintered (3D printed) nylon.

Designed by Walter Van Beirendonck, Belgian, b. 1957.
Woest man's ensemble, Winter 2017.
Jacquard woven polyester, acrylic, acetate, mohair, nylon.

Designed by Erin Robertson, American, b. 1987,
fabric designed by Jordan Piantedosi, American, b. 1988.
Protest Print Coat, 2017. Cotton and polyester plain weave,
embroidered with beads and sequins.

Rad Hourani, Canadian (born in Jordan), b. 1982.
Unisex Couture Look #3, Fall/Winter 2012.
Wool twill and leather.

Designed by Anvita Sharma, Indian, born late twentieth century,
for Two Point Two, Indian, founded 2017.
Unisex ensemble, 2019. Silk plain weave.

INDEX OF DONOR CREDITS

Gift of William Storer Eaton (41.887), 39

The Daphne Farago Collection (2006.418), 69; (2006.102), 243

Frank M. and Mary T. B. Ferrin Fund (2013.12), 215

Gift of Michelle Tolini Finamore in memory of Richard Finamore (2011.1790), 218

Gift of Marilyn Glass (2012.1043.1-2), 207

Gift of Mrs. Joseph W. Glidden (61.1251), 171

Gift of Lois Adams Goldstone (2002.696.1-5), 129

Gift of Harriet Wilinsky Goodman (1980.484a-b), 194

Marshall H. Gould Fund, funds donated by the Fashion Council, Museum of Fine Arts, Boston, and Susan Cornelia Warren Fund (2009.2841.1-3), 244–45

Gift of Jane P. Guild (1988.408a-b), 176

Bequest of Minna B. Hall (51.2361), 75

Gift of Susan Morse Hilles (53.2342), 212

Gift of the artist, HIRO (2002.159), 242

Gift of Philip Hofer, Esq. (63.2498), 97; (63.2525), 162

Gift of Mrs. Robert Homans (46.209a-c), 120; (46.207a-b), 121; (46.199a-b), 137; (46.204a-b), 139

William Morris Hunt Memorial Library, Museum of Fine Arts, Boston—The Elizabeth Day McCormick Collection (DT TT500.J6.8), 78

Gift of Miss Annie Jewett (13.586e), 47

Gift of Mr. and Mrs. Edward C. Johnson (63.1070a-b), 131

Ernest Kahn Fund (2006.1393), 241

Gift of Susan B. Kaplan (2008.264), 161

Bequest of Maxim Karolik (64.1910), 109

Gift of Mrs. Henry P. Kendall (64.1001a-b), 113; (64.1003a-c), 126

Bequest of David P. Kimball (23.504), 45

Gift of Irene Konefal in memory of Genevieve and Edmund Konefal (2010.684.1-2), 148

Gift of Lizbeth Krupp (2010.228), 277

Gift in memory of Mrs. Horatio Appleton Lamb (52.1155), 101; (51.36), 114

Gift of the artist, Helmut Lang (2009.4602.1-7), 286; (2009.4608.1-5), 287

The Evelyn H. Lauder Fashion Collection— Gift of Leonard A. Lauder (2017.4176.1), 272; (2017.4173.1-2), 290; (2013.707), 306

Leonard A. Lauder Postcard Archive—Gift of Leonard A. Lauder (2012.9129), 156

Gift of Mrs. James M. O'Neil in memory of her grandmother, Mary Ruby (1989.816), 183

Gift of Reva Ostrow (2013.1539), 179; (2009.2365.1-2), 193; (2013.1532), 200; (2009.2361.1-2), 206; (2013.1560.1-2), 210; (2013.1559), 211

Gift of Mrs. Norman J. Padelford (1972.911), 140

Museum purchase with funds donated by Rebecca Gold Milikowsky (2007.598.1-2), 283

Museum purchase with funds donated by Jane Pappalardo (2011.46), 198

Gift of Mrs. Harry B. Parmelee, in memory of her husband, Harry B. Parmelee (50.2705a), 100

John H. and Ernestine A. Payne Fund; (2010.589.1-2), 50; (2007.280), 225

Gift of Miss Mary Perdew (53.167a-b), 152, 153

Gift of Mrs. W. Y. Peters (50.2373), 151

Gift of Prada USA (2007.574.1-2), 299

Gift in memory of Helen Kingsford Preston (1989.347), 83

Gift of Herb Ritts (2000.885), 268; (2000.854), 276

Gift of Emily Welles Robbins (Mrs. Harry Pelham Robbins) and the Hon. Sumner Welles, in memory of Georgiana Welles Sargent (49.1015a-b), 88; (49.880), 89; (49.881a-d), 108; (49.1020a-b), 117

Gift of Karen Sethur Rotenberg in memory of Sylvia Sethur (2012.545), 229

Gift of the heirs of Bettina Looram de Rothschild (2013.1774), 135

Gift of Mrs. Edwina Curtis Rubenstein (53.97a-b), 166

Gift of Jody Sataloff in memory of Dr. Joseph Sataloff (2016.391), 147

Arnold Scaasi Collection-Gift of Arnold Scaasi. Made possible through the generous support of Jean S. and Frederic A. Sharf, anonymous donors, Penny and Jeff Vinik, Lynne and Mark Rickabaugh, Jane and Robert Burke, Carol Wall, Mrs. I. W. Colburn, Megan O'Block, Lorraine Bressler, and Daria Petrilli-Eckert (2009.4013.1-2), 230; (2009.4035.1-2), 231; (2009.4017.1-2), 235; (2009.4086), 250; (2009.4085.1-2), 251; (2009.4112), 270

Arnold Scaasi Design Drawings—Museum purchase with funds donated by Jean S. and Frederic A. Sharf (2009.4133.60), 239

Gift of Mrs. Hugh D. Scott (50.803a-b), 136

INDEX OF NAMES

mfa Museum of Fine Arts Boston

This work is published by arrangement with the Museum of Fine Arts, Boston. The MFA Boston mark is the exclusive trademark and service mark of the Museum of Fine Arts, Boston, and is used with permission.

First Edition
10 9 8 7 6 5 4 3 2 1
ISBN 978-0-7892-1380-8

Library of Congress Cataloging-in-Publication Data available upon request

For bulk and premium sales and for text adoptions procedures, write to Customer Service Manager, Abbeville Press, 655 Third Avenue, New York, NY 10017, or call 1-800-ARTBOOK.

Visit Abbeville Press online at www.abbeville.com.